The *AIRPLANE*
Alphabet Book

Jerry Pallotta
and
Fred Stillwell

Illustrated by
Rob Bolster

Charlesbridge

Extra special thanks to Shake

—J. P.

This book is dedicated to my grandchildren, Paul and Logan,
who share my enthusiasm for airplanes.

—F. S.

I dedicate this book to my wonderful wife, Elizabeth, who is a constant source of love and strength;
to my beautiful children, Carolyn, Allison, Luke and William; and to my family and friends; and especially to Jerry.

—R. B.

Text copyright © 1997 by Jerry Pallotta and Fred Stillwell
Illustrations copyright © 1997 by Rob Bolster
All rights reserved, including the right of reproduction in
whole or in part in any form. Charlesbridge and colophon
are registered trademarks of Charlesbridge Publishing, Inc.

Published by Charlesbridge
85 Main Street, Watertown, MA 02472
(617) 926-0329
www.charlesbridge.com

Printed by Sung In Printing in Gunpo-Si, Kyonggi-Do, Korea
(hc) 10 9 8 7 6 5 4 3 2
(sc) 15 14 13 12 11 10

Library of Congress Cataloging-in-Publication Data
Pallotta, Jerry.
    The airplane alphabet book/by Jerry Pallotta and
Fred Stillwell; illustrated by Rob Bolster.
        p.   cm.
    ISBN 978-0-88106-907-5 (reinforced for library use)
    ISBN 978-0-88106-906-8 (softcover)
1. Airplanes—Juvenile literature. 2. Alphabet—Juvenile
literature. [1. Airplanes. 2. Alphabet.] I. Stillwell, Fred.
II. Bolster, Rob, ill. III. Title.
TL547.P246 1997
629.133'34 — dc20
[E]   96-11360

The ability to fly is one of mankind's greatest achievements. For thousands of years, people have watched birds and wondered what it would be like to fly and to see the earth from above. People wished they could magically travel long distances in a short time or go over mountains without climbing or cross oceans without sailing on a long voyage. Many clever people attempted to fly in various contraptions over the years. Some tried balloons and some tried gliders. Finally, on December 17, 1903, in Kitty Hawk, North Carolina, Wilbur and Orville Wright flew the first "airplane."

Since the invention of the airplane, people can now fly.

Aa

A is for AT-6. The Aviation Trainer
Six is an important airplane because it was
used to train thousands of pilots all over the world.
Receiving a pilot's license is still a wonderful accomplishment.

Bb

B is for B-17. If you ever see an airplane with the letter *B* in its name, it means bomber. The B-17 was used in World War II to help the Allies win the war. This American plane was also called the Flying Fortress, and it usually flew with a crew of ten people.

Cc

C is for China Clipper. The China Clipper was a flying boat. In the early years of passenger flying, businessmen and famous people wanted to fly to faraway places. Many of these countries, such as China and India, did not have airports or runways. Who needs a runway when you can land in a harbor?

Dd

D is for Dauntless. The ever-increasing speeds of airplanes created a new problem: How to stop? Flaps were invented. The flaps slow a plane down when it is diving or coming in for a landing. The Dauntless had something new in its design—Swiss cheese flaps.

Ee

E is for Electra. The Electra has two tails. In wind tunnel tests, engineers figured out that this plane would go out of control in certain situations if it only had one tail. So it was redesigned with two.

Ff

F is for Ford Tri-Motor. This airplane has three engines. It was a popular plane for exploration because three engines are safer than one or two. In 1929 a Ford Tri-Motor with skis, instead of wheels, was the first airplane to fly over the South Pole.

Gg

G is for Gooney Bird. This airplane was a DC-3, a Douglas Commercial Three. At one time this airplane carried nine out of every ten air passengers in the United States. The Gooney Bird's other nickname was Sky Train.

GA 4676

Hh

H is for Hercules Flying Boat. This huge, all-wood cargo plane is also called the *Spruce Goose*. It only flew once, but it still holds the record for having the longest wingspan of any airplane ever built.

At one time, some engineers thought there would never be a metal airplane. Those pessimists were wrong. Today planes and jets are made with strong, lightweight metals such as aluminum and titanium.

I is for Invader. This warbird was usually painted black so it would be difficult to see during nighttime missions.

Flying at night and in terrible weather posed many problems. Instruments were invented: the directional gyro, the radar, the fuel gauge, the transponder, the altimeter, the air-speed indicator, the artificial horizon, the turn coordinator, and the vertical speed indicator. These instruments along with a clock and a compass allow pilots to fly safely without looking out the window.

Ii

J is for Jenny. The Jenny was a barnstorming plane. Huge crowds would come from miles around to see these traveling air shows. Barnstormer pilots earned their pay by doing wild stunts, such as walking on the wing, diving at the crowd, and flying loop-the-loops.

Don't try this at home!

Jj

Kk

Most airplanes have a propeller in the front. The propeller pulls the airplane and blows air over the wing. Each wing is shaped so that the air travels faster over the top of the wing than under the bottom of the wing. This causes lift. The wings of birds are shaped the same way.

K is for Kyushu. This airplane had a propeller on its tail.

LOW PRESSURE

AIRFLOW

AIRFOIL

AIRFLOW

HIGH PRESSURE

L is for Lightning. This famous airplane has a very unique design. It has one pilot, but it has two engines and two fuselages. The fuselage is the body of the plane, and the cockpit is where the pilot sits.

Mm

M is for Messerschmitt. These planes are looking for a dogfight. A dogfight is an aerial battle between two or more fighter planes while flying close to each other. The Messerschmitt was a German fighter plane in World War II.

It is common for fighter planes to fly in a V formation.

N is for Navy Duck. This seaplane does not quack, but it can take off from and land on the water. Instead of wheels, some planes have pontoons. A pontoon is a float that is attached to the airplane.

Oo

O is for Osprey. Is it a helicopter, an airplane, a jet with propellers—or is it a little of all three? This aircraft's radical design was developed so that it could take off vertically. Maybe it should not be in an airplane book. You decide!

While you are reading this book, some men and women are busy in the control tower directing air traffic.

P is for Piper Cub. Today almost anyone can fly a plane if they work hard, go to flight school, and get a pilot's license. Many people fly single-engine airplanes called Cubs. They may fly to work in another state, take a friend for a ride, or go sightseeing.

Pp

Qq

Q is for Queenaire. There is a passenger airplane called the Queenaire, but there is a more important Q.

Q is also for *Question Mark*. In 1929 aviation history was made when an Atlantic 2C-A airplane named the *Question Mark* flew nonstop for more than four days. It never ran out of gas because it was refueled while in flight. Pilots jokingly call this "passing gas."

Oh no! A plane crashed. Is anyone hurt?
Did the pilot survive? Were there passengers?
Did it crash into anyone's house?

We are sorry about the crash, but there is nothing to worry about. It was only a remote-controlled model airplane. Building and flying model airplanes is a great hobby.

R is for Ryan. In May 1927 Charles Lindbergh was the first person to fly a solo nonstop flight across the Atlantic Ocean. It was a remarkable feat, and he was an instant hero. He named his plane the *Spirit of St. Louis*. Look closely at the design of this Ryan airplane. It doesn't have a front window! Every inch of extra space was used to store fuel.

Rr

Ss

S is for Spitfire. What a great name.
Spitfire! Spitfire! Don't you just love saying it?

The British fell in love with this airplane. Its elliptical
wing made it maneuver slightly better than the
Messerschmitt, and eventually it ruled the skies over
Europe in World War II. The aircraft carrier version
was called the Seafire.

T is for Triplane. Engineers thought they could get just as much lift with three short wings as they could with one long wing. They were right. The Triplane did not fly as fast as a biwing or a monowing, but it did have an advantage. The short wings made it easier to store in a hangar. A hangar is a garage for an airplane.

Uu

U is for Ultralight. Have you ever seen these tiny airplanes fly over your neighborhood? They sound like giant bumblebees. Flying an Ultralight is as close as you can get to being a bird!

Vv

V is for Vega. Vega is the type of airplane that Amelia Earhart flew. In the early years of flying, not many women were pilots. Amelia Earhart was the first woman to fly solo nonstop across the United States. She was also the first woman to fly solo across the Atlantic Ocean. In 1937 Amelia Earhart disappeared over the Pacific Ocean in an Electra while trying to fly around the world.

Ww

W is for Wright Flyer. The Wright brothers' twelve-second flight made history because they accomplished three things at once. They flew a "heavier-than-air" craft, the plane became airborne under its own power, and Orville controlled the aircraft. Wilbur and Orville Wright would be proud to know that only sixty-six years later, astronaut Neil Armstrong brought a piece of the original Wright Flyer to the moon and back.

Xx

X is for Xingu. The Xingu is a Brazilian twin engine six-seater that is used to transport VIPs—*Very Important People.*

Whenever you see the initial *X* in the name of an aircraft, it usually means experimental.

Yy

Y is for Yak. No, not the mammal—the airplane! This Russian plane was named after Aleksandr Yakovlev, the man who designed it. It is much easier to call it a Yak than a Yakovlev, or a yackety-yak!

Maybe you will go to college, study aerodynamics, and design a plane someday, too.

Z is for Zero. During World War II, Americans had nicknames for enemy aircraft. The nicknames made it easy to identify the planes. Zero is the nickname of a Mitsubishi A6M fighter plane. There are a zillion other airplane nicknames, such as Barbara, Jill, Liz, Kate, and Nick.

What is that strange sound? Look up! There is a flying machine that has no propellers. How could this be? What is it?

Whatever it is, a new age is here . . .

JETS!